INT
70
S74L

14:

The Washington Papers

Strains in International Finance and Trade

Fred H. Sanderson
and
Harold Van B. Cleveland

a SAGE Policy Paper

$2.50
(£ 1.00)

The Washington Papers

are specially commissioned to bring you authoritative evalua-
tions of current developments in U.S. foreign policy and
world affairs. THE WASHINGTON PAPERS offer timely,
provocative, in-depth analyses by leading authorities—who
also suggest likely future developments and analyze the
policy implications of recent trends. Papers in the series are
written uuder the auspices of the Center for Strategic and
International Studies (CSIS), Georgetown University, Washington, D.C., and published for CSIS by SAGE Publications,
Beverly Hills/London. The editor of the series is Professor
Walter Laqueur, chairman of the CSIS Research Council and
director of the Institute of Contemporary History and Wiener
Library, London. Dr. Alvin J. Cottrell, CSIS Director of
Research, and M. Jon Vondracek, CSIS director of communi-
cations, are associate editors of the series.

14: Strains in International Finance and Trade

THE WASHINGTON PAPERS
Volume 2

14: Strains in International Finance and Trade

Fred H. Sanderson
Harold van B. Cleveland

THE CENTER FOR STRATEGIC AND INTERNATIONAL STUDIES
Georgetown University, Washington, D.C.

SAGE PUBLICATIONS
Beverly Hills / London

For information address:

SAGE PUBLICATIONS, INC.
275 South Beverly Drive
Beverly Hills, California 90212

SAGE PUBLICATIONS LTD
St George's House / 44 Hatton Garden
London EC1N 8ER

International Standard Book Number 0-8039-0443-6

Library of Congress Catalog Card No. 74-78422

FIRST PRINTING

*When citing a Washington Paper, please use the proper form. Remember to cite
the series title and include the paper number. One of the two following formats
can be adapted (depending on the style manual used):*

(1) HASSNER, P. (1973) "Europe in the Age of Negotiation." The Washington
Papers, I, 8. Beverly Hills and London: Sage Pubns.

OR

(2) Hassner, Pierre. 1973. *Europe in the Age of Negotiation.* The Washington
Papers, vol. 1, no. 8. Beverly Hills and London: Sage Publications.

CONTENTS

EDITORS' FOREWORD

This Washington Paper incorporates two studies on important current issues of international trade and finance. The study by Fred Sanderson is timely because it includes an analysis by the author of the impact of the energy crisis on American-European economic relations. In doing so, Mr. Sanderson makes reference to Secretary of State Henry Kissinger's proposal for technological collaboration between the United States and Western Europe in coping with problems arising from the Arab oil embargo.

The study by Harold van B. Cleveland is particularly notable for its extensive analysis of the theoretical aspects of international monetary problems, which he treats in both a contemporary and international context.

Coming at a time of increasing strain in the international economic system, the combination of these studies will contribute to public understanding of the problems at hand and the methods through which solutions can be found.

The Editors

PART ONE:

Economic Strains in the Atlantic Partnership

Fred H. Sanderson

I. A MOUNTING TIDE OF DISPUTES

Among the events that have shaped the history of the past quarter century, one stands out above all others. The Cold War; the Communist takeover of China, Korea, and Vietnam; decolonization; the rise of the Third World—all have made their imprint. But the most far-reaching development by far has been the undramatic process of construction of the great system of economic, political and military cooperation and interdependence among major industrial countries reaching across the Atlantic and Pacific. It is to the credit of the United States that it has provided leadership for the effort of reconciliation and reconstruction that has laid the basis of the postwar world order.

There are unmistakable signs that this proud edifice is beginning to crumble for lack of maintenance, repairs, and needed remodeling. It is not that the parties have decided upon reflection that the edifice is no longer needed or that living together has become intolerable: they all confess to seeing no viable alternative. But there is enough bickering over sharing the rent and observing the tenants' code to make life increasingly difficult for all concerned.

Dr. Kissinger (1974) may have dramatized matters a bit when he said, in his opening statement at the Washington Energy Conference, that the world is threatened with "a vicious cycle of competition, autarchy, rivalry, and depression such as led to the collapse of world order in the Thirties." Yet he was right in describing the disarray and the infighting among the industrial countries in the face of the challenge of the oil exporters as a grave danger to our prosperity and to the entire structure of international cooperation so laboriously constructed over the last generation.

It is not too late to put our house in order. Indeed, the two great crises of the last few years—the dollar crisis and the oil crisis—may have served a useful purpose by focusing attention on the creeping decay that had set in.

We must turn without delay to the urgent task of repairing, restructuring, and revitalizing our political and economic relations. This is essentially a matter of political will, as our leaders are prone to tell us. But it is also a "crisis of lucidity", as M. Ortoli put it in characterizing the current disarray of the European Community—a matter of sorting out and understanding, of regaining perspective and a sense of proportion on the issues that divide us.

Benefits and Problems of Economic Interdependence

It is one of the ironies of history that the most serious tensions within the Atlantic partnership have developed in the area of its greatest and most visible successes.

When the United States launched the Marshall Plan in 1948, it laid the foundations of the grand design for economic, political, and military cooperation that unfolded in the 1950s and early 1960s. This cooperation found its expression in a number of international agreements and institutions, notably the International Monetary Fund (IMF), the General Agreement on Tariffs and Trade (GATT), the Organization for European Economic Cooperation (OEEC), the North Atlantic Treaty Organization (NATO), the European Economic Community (EEC), and the Organization for Economic Cooperation and Development (OECD).

The economic benefits of this cooperation have surpassed the most optimistic expectations. Western Europe's aggregate real gross national product more than tripled during the ensuing quarter century while that of the United States doubled. The wide gap between American and European standards of living almost disappeared. The volume of trade more than doubled in the 1950s, and again in the 1960s; and the rate of trade expansion seems to be accelerating. The European currencies became freely convertible in the late 1950s, and this greatly stimulated the flow of capital in both directions. U.S. direct investments in Europe grew from less than $2 billion in 1958 to $30.7 billion (book value) at the end of 1972. European direct investment in the United States also increased, and now amounts to $10.4 billion. In addition, Europeans now own $28.3 billion in U.S. corporate stocks and bonds while U.S. citizens own $3.6 billion in European securities.

As barriers to trade and capital movements were reduced, the North Atlantic area became one highly interdependent economic region. Transportation, travel, communications, and the conduct of business throughout this vast area are now almost as easy and as commonplace as between regions of the same country. A large international capital market has emerged within which capital flows easily and swiftly.

The multinational corporation has been a major factor in this development. Drawing on the material and human resources of different countries, it has become a vehicle for spreading modern technology and marketing and management techniques.

This high degree of interdependence has brought new problems. Maladjustments in any one country—inflation or recession, balance-of-payments deficits or surpluses—affect economic conditions in other countries of the region more rapidly and to a greater degree than was foreseen by the architects of Bretton Woods and Geneva. The greater the progress in reducing barriers to trade and capital movements, the more difficult it has become for national governments to insulate their economies from the effects of economic policies in other countries, or to protect particular economic sectors against changes in their international competitive position.

National governments and the international institutions have not yet learned to cope with this high degree of international interdependence. The days are past when unemployment or inflation were accepted as acts of God. People have come to look to their governments to do something about these problems, and the sensitivity of the public to economic dislocations is heightened when they seem to originate abroad. The greater visibility of disturbances involving international trade and payments has something to do with this—who can argue about the trade deficit, the investment position, or the balance of payments of New York State in the absence of statistics to support the argument?

There are other reasons why international maladjustments continue to be of greater concern than maladjustments within the same country. Labor mobility across national borders is still rather limited, even in Europe. Resource transfers over prolonged periods from one country to another are not as readily accepted as would be the case between regions within a country. But most important is the lack of strong and generally accepted common rules and institutions that can be seen to govern international economic relations in an effective and even-handed manner.

Much of the acrimony that has accompanied recent economic disputes between Europe and the United States can be traced to a mutual feeling of being "done in" by the other side's taking advantage of the absence of rules or abusing weaknesses and inequities in the existing rules. Indeed, the European Community itself has not been free of similar tensions.

Major areas of friction have been the European Community's protectionist agricultural policy; preferential trading arrangements with a growing number of nonmember countries and, more recently, the conclusion of bilateral arrangements with oil-exporting countries; and the European Community's emerging industrial policy, which may adversely affect American export and investment interests.

Trade and investment problems have been compounded by exchange rate maladjustments. The growing overvaluation of the dollar during the 1960s caused American goods to become less competitive with foreign products both at home and abroad. Frustrations over our apparent inability to deal with this problem fuelled protectionist pressures in the United States. The Europeans chose to see the other side of the coin: America was spending beyond its means and Europe was called upon to finance the deficit.

The overvaluation of the dollar also stimulated the flow of direct investment from the United States to Europe, and this, too, gave rise to complaints on both sides of the Atlantic. American labor unions called for government measures to prevent the "export of American jobs". Europeans became uneasy about American corporations using overvalued dollars to "buy up European industry".

It took two parity realignments and the additional depreciation of the dollar in 1973 to correct this problem. Indeed, there are those who feel the shoe is now on the other foot: European industrialists are beginning to worry about the competitive advantage that an *undervalued* dollar may give to American exports. In the United States there are faint rumblings of discontent over foreign takeovers of American firms at "bargain prices". Trade issues, too, took a surprising turn when a sudden spurt of foreign demand for American farm products caused prices of grains and soybeans to triple and the United States imposed temporary export controls on soybeans to dampen speculation. The action predictably led to cries of anguish across the Atlantic and strengthened the advocates of European agricultural self-sufficiency who had always argued that America could not be counted upon as a reliable supplier. Americans in turn were asking whether it was fair to expect the United States to give absolute priority to food exports in times of shortage when it was treated as a residual supplier of farm products to Europe in normal times.

As time went on, the debate grew more bitter. Trade disputes that used to be safely confined to the business section of the press became the front-page stuff of high diplomacy. Issues that should yield to sober analysis and compromise have become encrusted with ideology. In Europe, economic protectionism has come to be dignified as the "cement" that holds the European Community together. Self-serving policies are represented as an assertion of the European "identity" vis-à-vis the United States. Trade preferences for European exporters are justified on the basis of special European responsibilities in the Mediterranean and in Africa. In the United States, necessary adjustments such as devaluation, and more questionable measures such as the subsidization of exports through the DISC (Domestic International Sales Corporation), are heralded as long-overdue reassertions of the American economic self-interest.

There is a danger that the escalation of economic issues may lead to actions and counteractions that could undermine the multilateral trade and payments system. The escalation is already spilling over into the political and security spheres. If not brought under control in time, these disputes may do serious harm to the health and cohesiveness of the Atlantic system.

The Arab Oil Crisis

As 1973 drew to a close, these issues were eclipsed by the sharp pains of the Arab oil squeeze. Once more the industrial countries were guided, in the main, by short-sighted nationalistic reflexes. Despite much talk, little had been done within the OECD framework—or in the European Community, for that matter—to prepare for a contingency that had become increasingly likely since the formation of the cartel of petroleum-exporting countries. In retrospect it appears that the outbreak of hostilities in the Middle East only hastened an event that would have materialized, though less abruptly, without the Arab-Israeli conflict.

The immediate reaction of each importing country was to look out for itself. World powers that in the past had reacted sharply to lesser threats to their economic lifelines could be seen vying for the favors of former client states that had only recently emerged from their protective wings. The fragility of the ties in both the European and Atlantic communities was cruelly exposed.

Will the industrial countries continue to undercut each other in their efforts to safeguard their energy supplies or will they heed Dr. Kissinger's call for a common energy policy? Here again, the French have taken the lead in stressing differences between European and American interests. Why should Europe not take advantage of its lack of commitments to Israel to work out a mutually beneficial special relationship with the Arab states? In view of its heavy dependence on Arab oil, does Europe have a choice? What effective assistance can the United States provide Europe in this situation? Such questions cannot be dismissed lightly. The truth is that the United States and Europe are paying the price of their lack of foresight—the price of a decade of neglect of their energy resources and technology.

No doubt the reasoning leading to a go-it-alone policy is persuasive to many Europeans. The trouble is that more than one can play a game that is likely to be self-defeating. There are few developments that could prove more costly and more disruptive to the industrial countries than a competitive scramble for oil supplies.

The oil crisis will have a profound impact on transatlantic economic relations. Already there are signs of panic in those industrial countries that are most heavily dependent on oil imports and most concerned about their ability to pay for them. Hence the frantic efforts by France, Britain, Italy, and Japan to conclude bilateral agreements to nail down oil supplies in return for industrial plants and equipment as well as sophisticated arms. The terms of these deals seem to involve even higher prices for oil than those exacted from the international companies.

This development is fraught with dangers to the multilateral trading system. If not stopped in time, it may lead to a relapse into the beggar-my-neighbor policies of the 1930s: barter deals, competitive devaluations, trade and exchange restrictions, export subsidies in various disguises—all in a desperate effort to balance the books with the oil exporters.

There may be other spillover effects. Other raw-material-exporting countries may be tempted to emulate the oil exporters. In the industrial countries, the oil crisis may lend new respectability to security and geopolitical arguments in support of protection. The U.S. decision to achieve self-sufficiency in energy as soon as feasible may serve as a model. The U. S. decision, to be sure, makes strategic sense because events have demonstrated that we cannot rely on supplies from the Middle East. It also makes economic sense, because domestic sources of energy that remained unexploited so long as oil was cheap will now become competitive. But dubious analogies now surely will be drawn to apply the lesson we learned to areas such as food, shipping, aircraft, computers, and other industries that can make a plausible case for their essentiality in the event foreign supplies are cut off. Few people will stop to reflect on whether it is reasonable to assume that U.S.-European relations will deteriorate to the point where one partner will cut off supplies to the other. The French position on nuclear energy is indicative of this tendency: its proponents seem to be more concerned about lessening Europe's dependence on American-enriched uranium— representing about one percent of Europe's energy consumption— than about its critical (45 percent) dependence on Arab oil. Agriculture and advanced technology are other examples of the lack of confidence in transatlantic cooperation for which "Gaullist" attitudes on both sides of the Atlantic must bear a share of responsibility.

II. ANALYZING THE ISSUES:
MUTUAL BENEFITS CLOUDED BY PASSION

The Means to Cope

How can we cope with this mounting tide of disputes? Part of the problem is the tendency, already noted, to take rigid ideological positions that are hard to reconcile, and to exaggerate the difficulties of mutual adjustment. The first prerequisite for making progress on these issues, therefore, is dispassionate analysis of what is really involved.

Take argicultural trade, which is the oldest bone of contention between the United States and the European Community. The Community's Common Agricultural Policy (CAP) maintains European grain prices at levels 50 to 100 percent above normal world market prices. This in turn raises the cost of meat and dairy products. The total cost to European consumers, in terms of higher prices, has been estimated (Atlantic Institute, 1970) at $8 billion for 1967; additional costs to taxpayers of national subsidies and payments to the common agricultural fund are of the order of $5 billion. As in the United States, the main benefits of high support prices have gone to large commercial farms which need them least.

There are misconceptions, on both sides of the Atlantic, as to the real nature of the issue. For example, European spokesmen like to point out that the CAP has not prevented a healthy expansion of American farm exports to the Community. However, the major factor in the continuing growth of these exports has been the spectacular boom in soybeans, which enter the Common Market free of duty in accordance with an earlier EC commitment negotitated in GATT in exchange for trade concessions by the U.S. Free entry of soybeans is the major remaining gap in the wall of protection surrounding European agriculture. Virtually all the growth in U.S. agricultural exports to the European Community since 1960 has been in soybeans.

American critics of European agricultural policy sometimes make it appear as if agricultural protectionism had been invented by the European Community. They forget that the national agricultural policies that were superseded by the CAP were, on the whole, equally protectionist in their effect, although the techniques of protection were different. It should also be kept in mind that the United States has a very high level of protection on some agricultural products; for example, the United States supports dairy products at higher prices than those prevailing in Europe even though U.S. prices of feedstuffs are much lower.

The American case in this dispute thus cannot be made in terms of superior virtue; nor can it be based primarily on the additional protection provided by the Common Agricultural Policy as compared with pre-existing national policies of the member countries. It rests, rather, on opportunities for gains in economic efficiency that a mutual reduction of agricultural trade barriers would make possible within the Atlantic region.

Fears of Liberalization: Opposing Ideologies

A major obstacle to even limited progress toward a gradual liberalization of agricultural trade stems from fears on both sides of the Atlantic over the consequences of such liberalization. A recent study by a U.S. Department of Agriculture team (1973) indicates that liberalization, far from "destroying" European agriculture, would merely mean a shift of emphasis from crop production to livestock production, with beneficial effects for all concerned. While European grain production would be less than under present policies[1], this would be offset by increases in beef and dairy production as consumption responded to lower prices and higher incomes. Europe would become a major dairy exporter. Farm employment would continue to decline, though probably not more, and possibly less, than would have been the case in any event. With fewer people on farms, per capita farm incomes would continue to rise. Agricultural producers in the United States and other agricultural exporting countries would benefit from increased export opportunities and somewhat higher world prices. Costs of farm programs in Europe as well as in the United States could be reduced sharply.

The study also indicates that the United States under free trade would become a major importer of dairy products. This frightens American dairy producers. But here again, the consequences of liberalization would be more benign than is generally believed. Dairy production in the United States is declining in any event because of increasing costs in the face of relatively inelastic demand. If foreign cheese and other dairy products were admitted more freely, some of the agricultural resources now devoted to dairy products (other than milk for direct consumption) would be shifted to satisfy rapidly increasing demands for meat and for feedstuffs to produce meat. Liberalization would merely speed up this process.

The debate over agricultural trade liberalization has been exascerbated and obfuscated by the ideological positions that have been taken. "Market organization" and "market orientation" have become battle cries in this confrontation.

The prevalent view in the European Community is that "agriculture is different" from any other industry. The Community accordingly advocates the extension of the system of fixed support prices to international markets. This approach requires negotiated market shares to the extent that price is no longer permitted to function as a regulator.

In the American doctrine, agriculture is not different—except perhaps in degree—from other industries facing problems of adjustment. Government assistance may be needed to prevent hardship and to facilitate adjustment. This should be done through measures that do not artificially stimulate production, impede consumption, or interfere with international trade.[2]

These ideological positions have their roots in differences in the weights the two sides give to various objectives, and differences in perceived interests. Dispassionate analysis would show, however, that the underlying differences are not as great as might appear from the sound and fury of the debate.

The American view sometimes stresses economic efficiency (comparative advantage) to the exclusion of other objectives. The European emphasis is on social and regional stability and on security of supply. It should not be beyond the power of human imagination to devise a system of domestic and international measures that reconciles these objectives. An approach along these lines would emphasize gradualism, to avoid any sudden disruption of customary ways of life. It would combine elements of "market organization" to prevent extreme market fluctuations (for example, agreements on jointly financed stockpiles and food aid) with a greater reliance on market forces in normal periods. It would provide for a gradual reduction of incentives to uneconomic production—though without necessarily changing the particular *techniques* of protection favored by different countries which are entrenched in existing legislation and institutions and therefore probably more difficult to change than the *levels* of protection. It would permit subsidies for limited social and regional purposes such as support of mountain farmers; and it would permit "production-neutral" payments to marginal farmers to enable them to take up other, more remunerative occupations on a part-time or full-time basis or to retire, and to provide them with an adequate minimum income for the adjustment period. Unlike price supports, such payments would generally be self-liquidating and, in any event, less costly than the present systems.

Facilitating Factors

There are several factors that should facilitate constructive solutions in this field. One is the world-wide inflation, which has led to increased concern about high food prices. The inflation also facilitates the gradual reduction of agricultural protection by making it possible to accomplish this objective without a reduction of nominal prices—a psychological factor of some political importance.

Another factor is the apparent change in the world agricultural demand/supply balance. Long-term projections are notoriously hazardous, and one should avoid drawing far-reaching conclusions from current shortages of agricultural products. High prices and the availability of efficient surplus production capacity in the United States and elsewhere make it likely that surpluses will recur in the 1970s. But there are reasons to believe that sometime in the near future the rising demand for more and better food that accompanies rising incomes may gradually put increased pressure on the world's agricultural resources and lead to a steady improvement in world markets for agricultural products. This should moderate the competition for markets and reduce the need for protection.

Finally, it should be borne in mind that the rationalization of agricultural production is already under way, not only in the United States but also in Europe. The exodus from farms is now more rapid in Europe than in America. European agriculture has been modernized and undoubtedly will be able to stand on its own feet some day, particularly if world food prices should gradually rise. This should make it easier for Europe to accept a gradual reduction of agricultural trade barriers.

Industrial Trade

In contrast with attitudes on agricultural trade, there has been a high degree of consensus on the desirability of freer industrial trade. The Community started out with a moderate average level of industrial tariffs (13.5 percent), which was reduced to about 8.5 percent in the Kennedy Rouud—matching similar reductions by the United States, Japan, and other industrial countries. But here, too, new issues are emerging that threaten to weaken this consensus.

Recent monetary instability has brought home the fact that exchange rate maladjustments can have more serious adverse effects on a country's international competitive position than foreign trade barriers or export subsidies. This new awareness of the interrelationship between trade and monetary relations has caused confusion on both sides of the Atlantic regarding the basic purposes of trade negotiations. Thus at the height of American frustration over the presumed impossibility of correcting the maladjustment between the dollar and other currencies, official U.S. spokesmen began to view the trade negotiations as a means of restoring balance-of-payments equilibrium. They accordingly called for unilateral, or at least more than proportional, reductions of trade barriers by other countries that were in balance-of-payments surplus. Now there is a feeling in Europe that the unexpected extent of the dollar depreciation that has taken place since 1971 has done enough to strengthen the U.S. trade position and that trade negotiations therefore should no longer be of great importance to the United States. This debate misses the main point of the trade negotiations.

To be sure, the United States and other nonmembers of the European Community do have a special stake in the trade negotiations: a multilateral reduction of trade barriers would reduce the discrimination against outsiders that is inherent in a customs union. Indeed, if *all* trade barriers were eliminated, nonmembers of the European Community would be on the same footing as members in competing within any EC country. A significant reduction of the Community's external tariff would also help to reduce the adverse effects which the establishment and enlargement of the Common Market may have on the trade balance of nonmembers. But, in the main, the economic case for trade negotiations must rest on the *mutual* benefits of expanded trade in promoting a better international allocation of resources, in stimulating competition and economic growth, and in facilitating the control of inflation (Brookings Institution, 1973).

There is an even more important consideration, which has to do with the economic and political dynamics of U.S.–European relations. It has often been said of the European Community that it must go forward if it is not to slide backward. This is equally true of the Atlantic partnership. The dangers of retrogression lurk not so much in the field of tariffs as in the vast and largely uncharted area of other government measures that can restrict and distort trade and investment flows. Preferential trading arrangements, import and export restrictions to prevent "disruption" of domestic markets, "buy American" and "buy European" policies in government procurement, "industrial policies" favoring high-technology industries, subsidies in the name of regional development, discriminatory restrictions on the dissemination of technology, restrictive technical, health, and safety standards, and restrictive rules of origin in European free trade arrangements all have a considerable potential for generating friction among the industrial countries. Proliferation of such measures—whether or not they are protectionist in intent—could easily undo the progress that has been made toward a freer and fairer world trading system.

Preferential Trade: A Disruptive Issue

Among these measures, perhaps the most hotly debated current issue concerns the European preferential trade arrangements with nonmember countries. It derives its significance not so much from the actual damage to American trade interests as from the challenge it presents to the most-favored-nation principle which is at the basis of the multilateral trade and payments system.

The EC has concluded or proposed preferential arrangements with over 50 countries in Western Europe, the Mediterranean, tropical Africa, and the Caribbean. The arrangements with European nonmember countries and Israel can probably either be justified as compatible with the free trade area provisions of the GATT, or modified to make them compatible. They cover industrial trade only, but industrial trade in these cases might be considered to constitute "substantially all the trade" between the EC and the countries concerned, as required by GATT.

The case for industrial free trade arrangements between the EC and developing countries, by contrast, is weak. Industrial free trade in these cases is essentially one-way and, in effect, a thinly disguised preference in favor of EC exporters at the expense of other industrial countries. Nor are such preferences in the interest of the developing countries concerned, as they limit the latters' freedom to choose the lowest-cost sources of supply. In any event these countries already have, or should have, duty-free access for their exports of manufactures under the generalized tariff preference scheme.

Just as it appeared that the Europeans might be prepared to concede this point, at least to the extent of abandoning their insistence on "reverse preferences" favoring European industrial exports, the issue has erupted again in the new context of European relations with the oil-exporting countries. Although the ostensible purpose of these arrangements is to secure European oil supplies, they also represent efforts to sew up opportunities to earn money to pay for the oil. The subsidized competition among state trading entities implied in these arrangements would seem to be incompatible with the European Common Market as well as with an open, nondiscriminatory world trade system.

Consistent with its traditional policy, the United States is attempting to slow down the bilateralist stampede and to bring the arrangements under a measure of international control. At a minimum, this should involve international consultations on the terms of the arrangements and restraints on open or hidden subsidies. Such trading rules should be buttressed by restraints on arms deliveries and multilateral arrangements to provide oil-exporting countries with profitable and safe opportunities for long-term investments in industrial and developing countries.

Industrial Policy: More Potential for Disruption

The European Community's "industrial policy" poses another potentially disruptive issue. Official pronouncements stress non-controversial aspects such as legal arrangements to facilitate mergers of European firms to put them in a better position to compete with the great American-based multinational corporations. American subsidiaries in Europe have been assured that they will continue to receive nondiscriminatory treatment; but as time goes on, the debate has taken on an anti-American flavor. There are indications that European firms in high-technology industries such as computers and aircraft may be favored by subsidies, research and development contracts, government orders, tax advantages, and special credit facilities. This would extend practices that already exist on a national scale to a Europe-wide scale. It has also been suggested that the Community's antitrust regulations might be administered in a discriminatory manner. Since the United States is relying increasingly on high-technology exports, where it has a comparative advantage, any measures favoring European production could damage American trade interests. Furthermore, any discrimination in favor of European firms and against American subsidiaries would affect U.S. investment interests. Both would have adverse effects on the U.S. balance of payments.

There are, at present, few international rules in this area. The Europeans like to point out that American high-technology industries have had the benefit of massive military and space programs, free use of government-developed technology, and "buy American" preferences for military procurement. There is a danger that the development of a European industrial policy may start a spiral of subsidies to industries in all industrial countries.

It is sometimes suggested that the answer to this problem may lie in joint ventures or other forms of cooperation between U.S. and European firms. While such arrangements have merit in some cases, they also raise questions concerning the maintenance of a healthy climate of international competition. A better approach would be to develop international rules on subsidies, including indirect subsidization through tax rebates, low-interest credit, and government procurement, and to strengthen existing provisions for the nondiscriminatory treatment of foreign companies.

There is reason to believe that the current antagonism toward the multinational corporations (which in any event is not shared by all Europeans) may subside in the years to come. The realignment of exchange rates will dampen the flow of U.S. investments to Europe and stimulate the reverse flow. As more European firms establish themselves in the United States, it will increase Europe's stake in rules to ensure the fair treatment of foreign investment.

The Divisiveness of Energy Requirements

The divisive potential of the energy problem should have been evident long before the oil crisis erupted in October 1973; nor should anyone have been taken by surprise at Europe's weak-kneed reaction to the Arab challenge. Western Europe is considerably more dependent on energy imports than the United States (60 percent as compared with about 15 percent). It imports virtually all of its oil (as compared with 30 percent for the United States), and a higher percentage of its oil imports comes from Arab countries (70 percent as compared with 40 percent). Thus the Europeans had even more reason than the United States to be concerned about a slowdown or cutoff of foreign oil.

Yet the governments were slow in facing up to the problem. Cooperation among major importing countries and oil companies to cope with the Arab supply and price squeeze was unequal to the pressure of demand in the industrial countries. Another factor favoring the exporter cartel has been the fortuitous fact that some of the key oil exporters are thinly populated underdeveloped countries that have little immediate need for additional revenue and are therefore readily disposed to take the lead in restricting exports.

Plans for sharing oil supplies in the event of an acute shortage likewise proved to be no match for the challenge when it materialized. At this writing the Western European members of the OECD have failed to implement their emergency oil-sharing agreement. The same is true of the "immediate measures" that the European Commission had urged on the members of the Community in October 1972 or the U.S. proposal to share overseas oil imports equitably among all OECD countries in the event of an emergency. Whatever sharing has taken place so far during the crisis seems to have been the result of efforts by the oil companies to apportion the shortage more or less equally among their regular customers.

Increased competition for oil supplies among industrial countries is probably inevitable for the remainder of the decade. Europe and Japan will continue to try to assure supplies through bilateral arrangements with individual oil-exporting countries. Such arrangements may take the form of long-term supply contracts combined with joint refining and marketing operations and joint investments in petrochemical and fertilizer plants. This approach will reinforce the trend in Europe toward strengthening the role of national oil companies. It will also lead to increasing interference with the operations of the international companies.

A proliferation of preclusive supply arrangements would probably further impair the bargaining power and worsen the terms of trade of the oil-consuming countries—although some might argue that it could also lead to increased competition among oil-exporting countries. Whatever the ultimate economic outcome, there can be little doubt about the additional strains such a development would impose on relations among industrial countries.

Over the longer term, the best defense of the industrial countries will be to speed up the development of their own energy resources and technology. High petroleum prices will provide the necessary incentive to intensify the search for domestic oil and gas and to turn to other sources of energy such as coal, shale, tar sands, nuclear power, and, ultimately, solar energy. And of course, higher energy costs should also result in more sparing and efficient use of energy.

Planning on both the national and international levels has been much too slow, considering the long lead time required for technological development and plant construction; fortunately, prospects are favorable for international cooperation in this area. The United States has the advantage of the most advanced technology and of relatively ample North American raw material resources. The required investments are so staggering, however, that the United States may have to call on European and Japanese capital to help develop these resources. Europe and Japan, in turn, can expect to gain from American technology in developing such resources as nuclear power and North Sea oil. These mutual benefits should provide a solid basis for the massive effort of financial and technical cooperation proposed by the United States.

But here again, smooth sailing is far from assured. One shoal that is already discernible is the incipient commercial rivalry in nuclear fuels and reactors. France, supported by Italy and Belgium, has made a strong bid for European self-sufficiency in enriched uranium based on a giant gaseous diffusion plant to be built in France. A British-Dutch-German consortium is working on a more modest program based on the cheaper and more flexible, but technically as yet less perfected, centrifuge technique. The latter approach would result in a more gradual buildup of European capacity and would require continued imports of enriched uranium from the United States well into the 1980s. The European Commission has endorsed the objective of European self-sufficiency and has proposed that members guarantee a market for whatever enriched uranium is produced in Europe. This leaves the United States in a quandary. Our enrichment capacity is now fully committed and since it takes six to eight years to plan and build new capacity, we need to know soon what European and Japanese requirements will be in the 1980s and beyond. A complicating factor is the emergence of the Soviet Union as a supplier of enriched uranium and reactors.

Future needs are so vast, however, that there should be ample room for contributions from all of these sources provided that the various national programs are kept in phase with each other. Appropriate international arrangements need to be worked out without delay. They should provide for long-term contracts and guarantees against discrimination between domestic and foreign purchasers, on a basis of reciprocity, as well as close cooperation in developing new technology.

III. FINDING A SOLUTION: NARROWNESS ABROGATED

The Tasks Ahead

Why do we seem to have such difficulties in dealing with international economic issues? There are many facets to this question but basically it comes down to the fact that, somewhere along the way, the determination on both sides of the Atlantic to build a closely knit system of economic and political relations slackened. We lost sight of our central purposes and got sidetracked by marginal and parochial short-term interests. Instead of strengthening OECD, GATT, and the IMF, we neglected these organizations and permitted their rules to be disregarded.

The shock of the energy crisis may provide an opportunity to reverse this trend. Although current European attitudes are not encouraging, there are some favorable factors.

The shakeup of the international monetary system should be entered on the positive side of the ledger. The realignment of exchange rates has strengthened the dollar and this has enabled the United States as well as Germany, the Netherlands, and Belgium to lift most of their restrictions on international capital movements. The United States had a trade surplus in 1973 and was approaching equilibrium in its balance of payments. The growing acceptance of more flexible exchange rates should help avoid the recurrence of persistent, massive imbalances among industrial countries.

A major problem now is the potentially unstabilizing effect on foreign exchange markets of excess reserves accumulated by oil-exporting countries. There are risks in unrestrained competition for these funds. The interests of all concerned would probably be better served by a multilateral approach. One possibility would be to provide oil-exporting countries with opportunities for both short-term and long-term investment that offer a measure of protection against exchange risks. This could be accomplished, for example, by creating a multilateral fund consisting of a composite of claims denominated in various currencies.

In the trade field, the most urgent matter is to prevent fears of massive balance-of-payments deficits because of increased petroleum prices from causing a relapse into economic nationalism. Beyond this, there remains the task of dealing with the remaining tariff barriers and with the proliferation of other government measures that distort international trade. A new problem in this area is the increasing tendency to resort to export restrictions. While export controls may sometimes be justified to deal with acute domestic shortages of foodstuffs, fuels, and materials, they should, like import restrictions, be subject to international rules and surveillance. In some cases, more far-reaching international arrangements to stabilize supplies and prices may be called for.[3]

Although the outlook for the trade negotiations remains clouded, there are some bright spots. Protectionist pressures in the United States may have passed their peak with the improvement in our trade balance. The spell of chauvinism that marred our foreign economic policy during the past few years seems to have passed. It is now likely that Congress will grant adequate authority to negotiate on tariffs as well as nontariff matters. In Europe, the French government in particular has shown some reluctance to go very far in dismantling trade barriers to the rest of the world. As matters stand, decisive moves toward freer trade and improved coordination of economic policies among industrial countries can be blocked or slowed down substantially by one or two EC member countries even though other members may be favorably disposed. Progress in this direction will continue to be hampered by long periods of stalemate as EC members try to reach agreement on common policies in new areas as well as by the ever-present temptation to settle their differences at the expense of nonmembers' interests.

The climate of the trade negotiations would be improved

considerably if governments could rise above their traditional narrow export-oriented motivations and give greater weight to the mutual benefits of economic interdependence in terms of economic efficiency and growth, consumer welfare, and good international relations. The growing articulateness of consumers in this age of inflation may help to nudge governments in this direction.

In the energy field, the United States has sketched out a sensible and constructive program for cooperation among consuming countries. While prospects for effective international coordination of supply and price policies are not bright for the short term, it should at least be possible to deal with the monetary and trade policy aspects of the problem. One would also hope that differences over short-term expedients will not be permitted to stand in the way of effective cooperation in developing alternative sources of energy, which is indispensable for a satisfactory long-term solution.

Active Coordination of Policies: An Imperative

The key to progress in all of these areas will be the willingness of the industrial countries to accept a much greater measure of international coordination of national policies than in the past. It is no longer sufficient to try to remove obstacles to the flow of trade and of capital. In an era of pervasive government intervention in economic affairs, joint problem management is an essential prerequisite for making a regime of interdependence work.

A good deal more is needed than the declarations of intent or the perfunctory process of consultation—too often after the fact—that have brought atrophy to so many international organizations. Problem management is a continual process of joint decision-making and adjustment of national policies. It is a difficult process, as the members of the European Community are finding out; it requires much more systematic, more timely, and more informed involvement of top policymakers in a large number of specific, tough policy issues. Excessive compartmentalization has hampered progress on such issues: it is a mistake to leave decision-making and negotiations on these matters largely in the hands of ministries and departments with special interests and limited horizons. Technicians and department heads are needed to sort out and analyze the issues, but only the top policymakers can provide the overview and leadership required to compromise and resolve them.

What is needed is a new way of doing things, not a new international organization. There is no lack of institutions and codes on which to build. The OECD has the potential for serving as the central forum in which the national economic policies of the industrial countries can be reconciled with each other and with the requirements of the international economic system. OECD would be the appropriate organization to deal with the energy problem, as the French have suggested (Jobert, 1974),[4] provided the industrial countries can agree on the basic principles of a common approach. IMF is uniquely equipped to ensure the proper functioning of a reformed internationl monetary system. In the trade field, GATT contains provisions concerning nondiscrimination, the establishment of customs unions and free trade areas, compensation for impairment of trade concessions, antidumping and countervailing duties, quantitative restrictions, subsidies, and emergency actions in the event of serious injury to domestic producers. Codes and understandings concerning invisible transactions, capital movements, and environmental policies have been developed in the OECD. Guidelines for government procurement, standards, export credits, investment incentives and restrictions, subsidies, and tax exemptions for domestic industries are under discussion in OECD and GATT.

These rules need to be spelled out and tightened—and they need to be enforced. The international organizations dealing with these matters need to be strengthened and their activities more closely interrelated. But, above all, national governments must see their way to subordinating short-term national preoccupations to their long-term national interest, which is to develop and uphold the rules and agreements governing their economic relations.

NOTES

1. Assuming that protection is phased out gradually over a period of 15 to 20 years, European grain production would continue to increase, although at a slower rate than under present policies.

2. Governments do not always practice what they preach. Thus the United States maintains nearly prohibitive restrictions on imports of dairy products. The U.S. Sugar Act may be regarded as a prototype of the European Community's approach to agricultural trade. The European Community, in turn, did not hesitate to compete aggressively in world wheat markets in the face of an international agreement to stabilize prices.

3. An outline of a code applicable to industrial countries has been put forward by the Atlantic Council of the United States (1974). See the Interim Report of Reform of the International Trade System.

4. French advocacy of the use of existing international organizations, rather than ad hoc "political" meetings, would carry greater conviction if France had not, more than any other country, obstructed decision-making and in some instances, even the discussion of controversial issues in OECD, IMF, and GATT.

26

REFERENCES

Atlantic Council of the United States (1974) Interim Report on Reform of the International Trade System. Washington, D.C. (February 11).

Atlantic Institute (1970) "A future for European agriculture," Atlantic Papers No. 4.

Brookings Institution (1973) World Trade and Domestic Adjustment, The Gains from Freer Trade (July).

French Foreign Minister JOBERT (1974) Statement at the Washington Energy Conference (February).

KISSINGER, H. (1974) Statement at the Washington Energy Conference (February).

U.S. Department of Agriculture (1973) Agricultural trade and the proposed round of multilateral negotiations. Report prepared for the Council on International Economic Policy, House Committee on Agriculture (April 30).

PART TWO:

The Prospect for International Monetary Order: An Historical and Analytical View

Harold van B. Cleveland

INTRODUCTION

Only a few years ago, the American dream of a unified, open, harmonious, and rapidly growing international economy seemed to have come true. In the decade from 1959 to 1968, the industrial world enjoyed the most rapid and stable economic expansion it had ever known. Exchange rates were stable and the inflation of the 1940s and 1950s had been left behind. World production, trade, and international investment grew at unprecedented rates. Although political relations among the Western allies were sometimes troubled, the source was not primarily conflict over economic or monetary issues.

Today, a very different picture meets the eye. The scene is one of growing conflict and disorder in international economic and monetary relations. We are in the midst of the worst peacetime inflation of modern times. Exchange-rate stability has broken down, exchange controls are proliferating, and the threat of trade controls looms ahead. Conflicts of economic interest among the industrial countries are weakening established political and military ties. And now the Arabs have launched a *jehad* against the industrial powers, with oil as the weapon, which could turn the world economic slowdown that was already in the cards into the worst recession of the postwar period. The losses of output and the added price inflation that may be caused by the Arab oil offensive will be temporary. But the conflicts it has engendered among the industrial countries could do lasting damage by reinforcing trends toward disintegration.

In this abrupt transition from order to disorder, monetary factors have played the central role. The postwar economy's earlier success was due in no small measure to the monetary system, based on the U.S. dollar, that emerged unplanned and somewhat unexpectedly after World War II. The present disorder and inflation can be explained in large part by the disintegration of the system.

An effort to understand the present state of international monetary relations and its probable outcome leads naturally to an examination of international monetary history. This is not the first time that a stable international monetary order has given way to disorder. The gold standard was also highly successful by the economic and political criteria of its day; but it, too, broke down spectacularly in the early 1930s, to the accompaniment of worldwide deflation, mass unemployment, and spreading exchange controls and trade barriers.

Why were the gold standard before 1914 and the dollar standard after World War II successful? Why did they break down? The critical factor in both cases seems to have been the presence—or absence—of centralized control of the international monetary base by a dominant power—Britain before 1914 and the United States after World War II. When such control was present, the system worked well. When the central power's control was challenged by a rival, or by the refusal of other powers to accept monetary leadership, the systems broke down.

This essay attempts to support this thesis with theoretical argument and historical evidence. The discussion is also intended to shed light on the perennial sources of trouble in international monetary relations and on the limits of the possible in monetary arrnagements among sovereign national communities. On this basis, an attempt is made to discern the probable evolution of the monetary system during the next few years and to offer a realistic judgment on the prospects for international monetary reform.

I. THE PROBLEM OF INTERNATIONAL MONETARY ORDER

To be orderly, an international monetary system must satisfy two criteria. On the one hand, exchange rates must normally be stable and exchange controls little used. On the other hand, the money supply of the countries participating in the system must grow rapidly enough to assure high employment, but not so rapidly as to cause intolerable inflation. In a world of sovereign nation-states monetary order in this sense is inevitably problematic, simply because the money supply is controlled at the national level, and with national interests uppermost, while at the same time the economic effects of each nation's monetary policy are by no means confined within its own borders.

If exchange rates are stable and there are no exchange controls, one country's monetary policy affects in some degree the pace of money growth in other countries, the degree depending upon the relative economic size of the countries in question. And since the level of employment and the rate of inflation depend on the rate at which a country's money supply is growing, no country, uuless it is very large in economic terms, is able to determine for itself these politically critical economic conditions. Other countries will have much less autonomy in this respect, and a small country will be entirely unable to manage domestic demand. Inevitably, therefore, national governments will confront difficult political choices from time to time—choices between exchange-rate stability and freedom of trade and payments on the one hand, and the maintenance of domestic employment or price stability on the other hand. Domestic political pressures will at times force governments to sacrifice stability and freedom of international exchange to the national interest in employment or price stability. Or, if priority is given to stable exchange rates and freedom of exchange, it will entail loss of control of domestic monetary conditions and the possibility of "importing" serious inflation or deflation.

This is true, at any rate, unless there exists some international or supranational mechanism which coordinates monetary expansion in the countries participating in the system, while at the same time maintaining politically acceptable rates of money growth in all countries. Yet a mechanism of this kind is itself highly problematic politically, for it presupposes the subordination of national monetary authorities to the agency or government that controls the mechanism. Such is the problem of international monetary order. Its essence is political: Who controls the world money supply and in whose interest?

These generalizations are rooted in contemporary monetary theory of the "monetarist" or "neo-quantity" persuasion. A little theoretical background may therefore be helpful in understanding them.

Money: National and International

There is at any time a certain "demand for money" in a national community—a certain total amount of cash that the members of the community desire to hold. This total bears a more or less stable relation to the community's aggregate income and expenditure. If, for example, the total stock of money is made to grow faster, there will be, for a time, an excess of cash balances over the amount the public desires to hold. As a result, the public will step up its rate of spending on financial assets (securities and bank deposits) and on real assets (goods and services) in an effort to restore the desired distribution of its wealth among cash, financial assets, and real assets. The resulting flows of money into the various credit markets and into the markets for real assets will cause the community's income to rise to a level that restores equilibrium between the actual and desired stock of money. If at the time the country's stock of money begins to grow faster its economy is operating well below full employment, the rise in total spending will mainly affect output and employment. But if the economy is already close to full employment, the effect will be mainly to raise prices. The rise in expenditure will be largely dissipated in inflation, without much effect on output. It follows that he who controls the growth of the money supply controls the growth of the national income and expenditure and, accordingly, of economic activity and prices.

In most countries, there is a rather stable relationship between the "monetary base", consisting of currency in circulation plus bank reserves, and the total stock of money or money supply in the hands of the public, which includes bank deposits as well as currency. In modern conditions, the central bank controls the monetary base, since it normally has the exclusive right to issue currency and can determine the level of bank reserves by buying and selling domestic securities and by making advances and discounts to commercial banks. It can also control the banks' reserves by buying or selling foreign currencies or gold in exchange for local currency, on the exchange market.

If, however, the country participates in an open international monetary system in which central banks are obliged to maintain exchange rates at official parities, a central bank's control of the national monetary base is far from complete. This is because monetary developments in the rest of the world will determine in greater or lesser degree the central bank's purchases or sales of foreign currencies or gold and thus additions to or subtractions from the country's monetary base coming from this source. If the country is small, the evolution of its monetary base will be almost entirely determined by monetary developments abroad. The appearance of control by the central bank will be illusory.

This is how it works. Suppose, for example, the monetary base in a number of countries begins to grow faster. Temporarily, there will be an excess supply of money in these countries. In time, the excess will be absorbed by a rise in spending, in business activity, and in prices in these countries. Meanwhile, however, some of the excess will be spent on financial assets and goods and services in countries where the growth of the monetary base has not accelerated. There will be, in other words, additional foreign demand for such countries' financial assets and goods and services, and a corresponding increase in demand on the exchange markets for their currencies to buy those assets, which have now become more readily available or cheaper than in the rest of the world. As a result, there will be a net flow of funds into these countries' monetary systems; that is, they will have a balance-of-payments surplus and the rest of the world, a deficit.

This international flow of funds will put pressure on exchange rates. To keep exchange rates from rising above or falling below official parities, central banks will intervene in the exchange markets, buying or selling the national currency for foreign currencies. In so doing, they will increase or reduce the local monetary base. And the smaller the country, the larger the proportionate effect on its monetary base.

International Money

Now, it is apparent that if countries wish to keep their exchange rates stable, central banks must dispose of ample reserves of some form of international money—i.e., a medium of exchange widely acceptable by foreigners—with which to finance balance-of-payments deficits and support their currencies on the exchanges. Countries that lack ample reserves will be forced to choose between domestic deflation and allowing their exchange rates to fall whenever their domestic money supplies begin to grow faster (relative to the demand for money) than the money supply is growing in the rest of the world.

But the possession of ample reserves by a country or countries is itself problematic—politically—for the rest of the world, at least if the country is large; for ample reserves give a country the possibility of financing large payments deficits, thereby enlarging other countries' monetary bases and perhaps undermining their attempts to fight inflation by holding down domestic monetary expansion. Moreover, a country that is able to finance large payments deficits is also able to extract a margin of real resources from the rest of the world in the form of an excess of imports over exports. Its real income is thereby increased at the expense of other countries' income.

If countries hold reserves in the form of financial assets denominated in other countries' currencies—as indeed they must unless the only kind of money in circulation is commodity money (gold or silver)—a further problem arises; for government and banks, including central banks, are not normally willing to accumulate large amounts of other countries' currencies, owing to the exchange risk involved in holding financial assets denominated in foreign currencies. Moreover, when a central bank acquires foreign currencies in large quantities as reserves, or permits private banks to do so, it relinquishes to that extent control of its domestic monetary base to foreigners and also finances a transfer of its real resources abroad.

For these reasons a monetary system that depends for international liquidity on reserves of national currencies is inherently problematic. A system of this kind, which might be called a multicurrency standard, will either have a strong deflationary bias, owing to the inadequacy of reserves to support fixed exchange rates, or its exchange stability will break down and exchange controls proliferate, as countries attempt to avoid deflation by an uncoordinated expansion of their domestic monetary bases.

To illustrate, let us imagine a monetary system consisting of a number of small and medium-sized countries that wish to keep their exchange rates stable and their exchange markets largely free of control. Each country's international reserves include a mixture of foreign currencies—those, let us say, of the two or three countries with the best record of exchange-rate stability and that have money and capital markets capable of providing financial assets sufficiently liquid and free of risk to be suitable for investment of central bank reserves. However, international reserves are kept small, owing to the exchange risks involved in holding foreign currencies—i.e., the absence of a really secure store of international value.

Now suppose that one of the larger countries suffers from excessive unemployment. It undertakes a program of public works, leading to a large budget deficit that is financed by the central bank through the open market purchase of securities. The resulting expansion of the country's monetary base will, *inter alia*, cause residents to demand more foreign exchange. The country's balance of payments will fall into deficit and the exchange rate will come under downward pressure. The central bank will be forced to sell a part of its slim reserves of currencies to support the exchange rate.

Foreign central banks will be reluctant to help out by buying the country's currency because of the exchange risk involved, or because they fear that they will thereby expand their monetary bases too rapidly and "import inflation". If they do nevertheless buy the foreign currency in order to keep their exchange rates from rising, they may "sterilize" the resulting increase in their reserves, so far as its effect on the domestic monetary base is concerned, for example, by open market sales of securities. The effect will be to prolong the difference in monetary conditions that was the cause of the payments imbalance.

In these circumstances, traders in the exchange markets will probably conclude that a devaluation of the first country's currency is likely and start selling it off in large quantities. Foreign central banks, too, may join in this speculative activity, selling off reserves of the weak currency in exchange for foreign currencies that seem likely to be revalued upward. At this point the country, if it wishes to maintain its exchange rate, will have to throttle back the expansion of its monetary base to about the same rate (relative to the demand for money) as in the rest of the world.

An international monetary system of this kind is thus liable to deflation if countries give priority to exchange-rate stability, and to unstable exchange rates if they give priority to domestic considerations. This is the fundamental problem of order in a world of national monetary systems.

Single-Currency Standards

In principle, there are two ways in which this Gordian knot could be cut. One is to subordinate national central banks to a supranational monetary authority—a central bank of central banks. National central banks would hold the superbank's liabilities (deposits or securities) denominated in a world currency of some kind, as international reserves. Since the superbank's liabilities would be free of exchange risk and could bear a competitive rate of interest, they would replace national currencies as international reserves. As a result, the superbank would be able to control the monetary base in each country by making advances or discounts to national central banks and by open-market operations in securities denominated in national currencies or perhaps in the international currency. It would accordingly have the power to assure a sufficient expansion of the world's monetary base and, at the same time, to keep national monetary policies sufficiently in line with each other to prevent large payment imbalances from arising. Countries would have sufficient international reserves, as well as access to credit from the superbank, to finance such deficits as might occur. But their reserves would not be so large as to put them in competition with the superbank as a source of international liquidity and a center of monetary control.

However, a supranational central bank presupposes a supranational political community. That may come to pass one day in Western Europe, remote as it seems today, but it is obviously irrelevant to the problem of monetary order on a global scale.

The other logically possible means to international monetary order is also the only one that has existed historically since the appearance of modern banking and national monetary systems. It is the subordination of national monetary systems to the monetary system of a dominant power and the use of its national currency as the most important component of international reserves and a major source of each country's domestic monetary base.

This was the nature of the gold standard—it was actually a sterling-gold standard—and of the post-World War II dollar system. In their mechanical details, the two systems differed significantly, reflecting the very different circumstances of the times. Yet both had in common the use of one national currency, which was regarded as being free of exchange risk because it was "as good as gold", as international reserves. The control of the supply of pounds by the Bank of England and of dollars by the

U.S. Federal Reserve System provided the necessary coordination of money growth throughout the system, and the use of one rather than a number of national currencies as reserve assets avoided the inherent weaknesses of a multicurrency standard.

So much, then, for theory. Let us now take a close look at the workings of the historical gold standard as it existed before 1914.

II. HOW THE GOLD STANDARD REALLY WORKED

T he textbook model of the gold standard describes a system
that is impersonal, automatic, and politically symmetrical.
There is no center. Each country plays a similar role. Gold is the
sole component of international reserves and the principal or
controlling component of each country's monetary base. Thus
the evolution of the world's monetary base is determined
impersonally and apolitically by world production of gold, while
national money supplies are kept in line by international gold
movements. If the money supply happens to grow more rapidly
in one country than in the rest of the world, its resulting
payments deficit will cause its banking system to lose gold to
other countries, and money supplies will come into line again.

As a factual description of how the historical gold standard
worked, this body of theory is misleading. Lacking the means to
enlarge the monetary base in particular countries or in the world
as a whole by discretionary monetary policy, a system of this
kind would have proved harshly deflationary whenever for any
reason—a crop failure, for example, or a political distrubance—a
country lost a lot of gold. A system of the sort described by the
economic texts could hardly have been as successful as the
historical system was if it had operated as automatically as
described. As Robert Skidelsky (1973) puts it:

> This theory of the [gold-standard] system was created after the first
> world war when it had ceased to function properly. It was less a
> scientific explanation of how it worked than an ideology with a
> clear purpose: to act as a central line of defense of *laissez faire*
> against socialism at home and protectionism abroad. Had the gold
> standard in fact operated in the way described it would, as Polanyi
> remarks, rapidly have reduced national economies to a heap of

ruins. That it did not do so can be largely explained by power relationships obscured by the theoretical descriptions. The automatic harmony of interests postulated by theorists was in fact imposed by Britain. The pre-1913 standard has been rightly described as a "sterling-exchange" standard or a "British-managed" standard. It was far from being automatic.

Economic historians have yet to describe the gold standard in terms of modern monetary theory, but it may have worked about as follows.

The monetary base in gold standard countries consisted in large part of the note issue, which was tied by a customary or legally required reserve ratio to the central banks' gold reserves. The base also included the gold holdings of commercial banks, their deposits with the central bank, and—most importantly for the present discussion—short-term assets denominated in sterling, such as bills of exchange drawn on British firms and deposits in London banks. Before World War I, sterling was not a reserve currency in the present-day sense; that is, it was not widely held by central banks. Nevertheless, it functioned as international reserves and "base money" by virtue of its importance in the portfolios of commercial banks throughout the trading world.

National money markets in gold-standard countries were all rather closely linked to the much larger London money market since neither exchange risks, which were normally absent, nor exchange controls impeded the movement of money between London and lesser financial markets abroad in search of the best return. At the same time, interest rates in the London money market were heavily influenced by "Bank rate", the Bank of England's discount or lending rate; for the Bank's advances and discounts, forming as they did a large and controllable part of the British monetary base, could exert a powerful impact on British commercial banks' own lending activities and thus on the total supply of sterling credit and its price.

Thus when Bank rate was raised, London money-market rates would also rise and funds would be drawn from other countries to London. Banks in other countries would accordingly lose reserves as their sterling assets diminished. If the outflow was sufficient to move the country's exchange rate against sterling down to the gold export point, gold, too, would flow to London. Credit restriction by the Bank of England would lead to credit restriction in other countries, with a corresponding impact on the growth of the local money supply.

Conversely, when the Bank of England decided to ease credit and lowered Bank rate, interest rates in London would fall and funds would flow out to other money centers. As a result, foreign banks' holdings of sterling assets would rise. If the expansion of credit in Britain was large enough in the circumstances to cause the exchange rate of the pound to fall to its gold export point, gold would flow out, too. With their reserves thus increased by the acquisition of sterling assets and perhaps gold as well, foreign banks would proceed to expand their loans, pushing local interest rates down and expanding the money supply in parallel with similar changes taking place in Britain.

Central banks, where they existed, were involved in this process, but their role did not differ essentially from that of commercial banks. In this period, central banks still operated in much the same way as commercial banks, apart from their responsibility as banks of issue to maintain the convertibility of the national currency into gold. They were often still privately owned or only quasi-public. Operating with little or no governmental interference, they did not usually consider it their responsibility to make an independent judgment, based on considerations of national economic advantage, whether or not to respond to what was happening in London. Nor were central banks charged with responsibility for defending the exchange rates of their currencies on the exchange markets. The maintenance of gold parities had, of course, the effect of keeping exchange rates within their gold points with respect to other gold-standard currencies. But this was not exchange stabilization in the interwar or present-day sense.

But the entire complex mechanism depended critically on the central banks' behaving as profit-making institutions, without government interference. When central banks began to accept a regular responsibility for supporting the public debt, for stabilizing exchange rates, and for helping to manage the domestic economy, the days of the gold standard were numbered. For these obligations were bound to come into conflict with the coordinating mechanism just described.

World War I and its aftermath of social change swept away the political bases of the pre-1914 gold standard—laissez faire and Britain's dominance in world trade and finance. Britain's economic decline and America's rise undermined Britain's central position, while changes in social forces and economic values and the disruptions of war and inflation forced governments and central banks to assert their control over exchange rates and the national monetary base. Monetary policy in the present-day sense was born, altering irreversibly the problem of international monetary order. Henceforth, order would be possible only in a system that compelled central banks, despite their new responsibilities, to follow policies conducive to payments equilibrium. Such a system would come into existence after World War II. Meanwhile, the international monetary system would pass through a purgatory of disorder and deflation.

III. AN EXPERIMENT THAT FAILED

I n his monumental historical work, *The International Gold Standard Reinterpreted,* William Adams Brown (1940: ii, 731) sums up the monetary history of the interwar years in the phrase, "the experiment of the gold-exchange standard without a focal point." During the 1920s the gold standard evolved into the gold-exchange standard, a form of multicurrency standard that lacked effective central control. The United States went its own monetary way and the dollar emerged as an international rival to sterling, while France resisted what it saw as the pretensions of both Anglo-Saxon powers to monetary hegemony. The system survived through the 1920s, living on the momentum of the past, and then broke down, contributing in the process to the worst depression of the twentieth century. In September 1931, sterling was forced off the gold standard and the ill-fated experiment came to an end.

This watershed in monetary history marks the end of serious efforts to restore a global monetary system based on fixed gold parities and the beginning of a phase of unstable exchange rates and currency blocs organized around the leading currencies. Born of depression and soon to be overtaken by the second world war, the new system never had a chance to demonstrate whether or not it was capable of achieving tolerable international monetary order.

Two Fateful Changes

The altered economic and political environment after World War I found expression in two changes in monetary institutions that affected profoundly the workings of the system. One was the establishment of the Federal Reserve System in 1913. (Prior to 1913, the United States had been without a central bank.) The other was the metamorphosis of the gold standard into the gold-exchange standard.

The possession of a central bank transformed the United States from a passive participant into a leading actor on the international monetary stage. Already the largest economic power, it was now a formidable monetary power as well, capable of exerting more deliberate influence on the world's monetary base than the Bank of England. The sheer size of the U.S. economy, as well as its large gold reserve accumulated during the war and its aftermath, gave the United States potentially more monetary autonomy than the other leading financial powers, France and Britain. The Federal Reserve was better able to offset the effect of a payments surplus or deficit on the domestic monetary base—as well as to finance a payments deficit—than the Bank of France or the Bank of England. Moreover, because the American economy was largely self-contained and the American banking system mainly oriented toward the credit needs of domestic business, the Federal Reserve Board took from the beginning a parochial, inward-looking view of its job, in sharp contrast to the imperial, international orientation of the City of London and the Bank of England.

The emergence of the gold-exchange standard—more precisely, the gold-sterling-dollar standard—was in origin a response to continental Europe's postwar shortage of gold. The European inflation during and after World War I had seriously reduced the purchasing power of Europe's depleted gold reserves, since gold was still valued at prewar parities. At the same time, Europe's need for international reserves was swollen by war damage to European industry and agriculture and by extraordinary import needs for relief and reconstruction. In principle, the shortage of gold would have been overcome by a large multilateral devaluation of currencies in terms of gold. But that was out of the question for European governments, whose intention was to restore the convertibility of their currencies into gold at their prewar parities as soon as possible. It was of no interest to the United States, which had more gold than it needed.

The remedy found by continental European central banks was to hold short-term foreign assets, such as treasury bills and bank deposits, denominated in sterling and to a smaller extent in dollars, as supplementary international reserves, against which the central bank could issue local currency and which could also be used to stabilize the European currencies on the exchanges. This practice had developed on an emergency basis during the war, but its continuation in peacetime was a major departure from tradition. Seen at the time as a technical device for "economizing gold", it proved to be a fateful alteration of the world's monetary system. It made possible a much more rapid expansion—or contraction—of the world's monetary base than could occur under the traditional gold standard. Sterling, dollars, and gold coexisted uneasily as reserve assets, establishing what we have called a multicurrency standard with the shortcomings already pointed out.

The Great Deflation

A detailed account of the international monetary history of the interwar period is beyond the scope of this essay. Instead, we shall zero in on one major episode, the extraordinary deflation that wracked the world economy from 1929-1933. Recent monetary histories of the period lay the chief blame for the depression at the door of the U.S. monetary authorities; but the inherent shortcomings of the gold-sterling-dollar standard, and the conflicting monetary policies followed by the other main actors, Britain and France, greatly amplified the consequences of the Federal Reserve's harshly deflationary policy. French gold policy, in particular, may have played a larger role than U.S. monetary policy in bringing on the catastrophe.

For four years, from January 1928 until February 1932, the Federal Reserve pursued a severely restrictive monetary policy. Its impact was highly contractionary abroad as well as at home. U.S. capital exports ceased and large inflows of funds and gold developed, putting strong downward pressure on the monetary base of the rest of the world. Moreover, under a policy adopted in the early 1920s (when gold inflows had also been large) and still in effect, the gold inflow was not allowed to enlarge *pro tanto* the U.S. monetary base. It was partly sterilized, in order to reinforce the Fed's tight money policy. As a result, the flow of gold to the United States did not simply shift base money from Europe to America; it helped bring about a net contraction in the world's monetary base.

Unfortunately, the monetary and exchange-rate policies of Britain and France, far from mitigating the deflationary impact of the Fed's policy, reinforced it. In 1925, the pound had been restored to its prewar parity, which left it overvalued relative to the French franc and the dollar. The following year, the franc was stabilized de facto at a level that undervalued the French currency not only against the pound but also the dollar, and this exchange rate was confirmed in 1928 when the franc was put back on the gold standard. This exchange-rate pattern contributed to the general deflation in several ways. British exports languished, and the Bank of England was forced to follow a generally restrictive monetary policy in order to safeguard as far as possible its gold reserve and to increase confidence in sterling; for the Bank of England and the British financial community were determined to restore as far as possible the City of London's prewar financial predominance. The pound's overvaluation and Britain's restrictive monetary policy were responsible for a long period of economic stagnation and high unemployment in Britain.[1] Thus, when the Fed's restrictive policies began to slow the U.S. economy down, the British economy—then the world's second largest after the United States—was already depressed.

As for France, the franc's undervaluation kept French exports growing rapidly and industrial output rising until 1930. Funds were drawn in from abroad, which allowed the French monetary base to expand sufficiently to keep domestic output expanding but aggravated the downward pressure on the monetary base in other countries. Moreover, the inflow pushed the franc up to its gold point against sterling and the dollar, resulting in a large inflow of gold. The French authorities—partly as a result of institutional rigidities in the French monetary system, partly as a matter of policy—sterilized a large portion of the gold inflow. The contractionary effect of this policy on other countries, including Britain and the United States, was compounded by the decision of the French authorities in 1928 to abandon the gold-exchange standard and to convert, to the extent possible, the Bank of France's sizeable holdings of sterling and dollars into gold.

French policy in this period had two aims. One was to acquire sufficient gold to restore a high ratio between the gold holdings of the bank of France and the domestic note circulation. (Traditional French monetary doctrine holds that the value of a fiduciary currency depends not on its supply relative to the demand for it—a view which has been the centerpiece of Anglo-Saxon monetary theory since Ricardo's classical formulation—but rather on its gold "backing".) The other aim was resistance to Britain's—and later America's—monetary hegemony.

These two preoccupations come together in the longstanding French distrust of the gold-exchange standard. Although in the early 1920s France was forced by its shortage of gold to use sterling assets as monetary reserves, it distrusted the system on both political and economic grounds. The French authorities saw it as an effort by the City of London to restore its pre-1914 dominance of world finance and as an engine of inflation, by which the Bank of England could force an expansionary monetary policy on France by the simple expedient of expanding credit in Britain. Many years later, President Charles de Gaulle, speaking of the dollar rather than the pound, was to echo these sentiments. His Finance Minister, Valéry Giscard d'Estaing, once referred to the gold-exchange standard by its English name, adding that this *"terme bizarre"* was so un-French as to have no equivalent in the French language.

Britain's abandonment of the gold standard in September 1931 and the subsequent downward float of the pound proved to be good medicine for Britain's ailing economy. It enabled the Bank of England to follow an expansive monetary policy, and as a result deflation in Britain in the 1930s was never as severe as on the Continent and in the United States. But the external repercussions of sterling's fall for the United States and France only worsened the general deflation. Confidence in the dollar weakened, and there was a massive withdrawal of European funds from New York, while European central banks proceeded to cash in their remaining dollar reserves for gold. The result was another round of contraction of America's and the world's monetary base. Base money was destroyed in large quantities at precisely the moment when the world, in the early stages of a depression caused by the earlier monetary restriction, needed monetary expansion. As a result, an ordinary business recession developed into a disaster of epic proportions. The pound's fall in September 1931, followed 18 months later by the devaluation of the dollar, left the French franc and the other continental currencies still tied to gold high and dry—substantially overvalued relative to the pound and the dollar. It was then these countries' turn to feel the full impact of the world deflation. Unemployment rose and France's recovery from the depression was seriously delayed. It did not fairly begin until 1936, when France was finally forced to abandon the gold standard and allow the franc to fall against the dollar and the pound. The franc's fall was not due to a change in French monetary philosophy but to the domestic political reaction to deflation and unemployment. It was Leon Blum's Popular Front government and its expansionary domestic policies that finally brought the franc down.

Remote as all this seems today, it is difficult to write about the policies that were so largely responsible for the Great Depression without a note of criticism. But that is not the point of this brief historical review. The point is rather to bring out the structural weaknesses of the interwar monetary system: first, the potential for disorder in a system where the control over the world's monetary base is divided, because the three leading countries are able to pursue independent monetary and exchange-rate policies; second, the potential for deflation inherent in a multicurrency standard, where countries are determined to maintain fixed exchange rates.

A New Kind of System

The pound's fall marked the beginning of the end of the long and futile effort by the major powers to restore a unified global monetary system with fixed gold parities, and the beginning of a period of currency blocs organized around the leading financial powers. Between the blocs, exchange rates were unstable and exchange controls and import restrictions were used to cope with payments imbalance.

Sterling after the fall was managed rather flexibly vis-à-vis the dollar and the franc by the British Treasury's Exchange Equalization Account (established in 1932), in a manner reminiscent of the pound's "dirty float" today. A large part of the world had pegged its currencies tightly to sterling after September 1931, so a globe-encircling sterling bloc came into being alongside a dollar bloc that included the United States and its possessions, part of Latin America, and, more ambiguously, Canada. A third bloc formed in Western Europe under French leadership: known as the gold bloc, it consisted of France, Belgium, Holland, Switzerland, Italy, and a few East European countries that clung to their old gold parities after the pound went off gold and the United States devalued. When the franc was forced off the gold standard in 1936, the other gold bloc members pegged their currencies to the French franc. Germany, for its part, though its currency remained nominally on the gold standard at the old parity, was constructing a bloc of its own in Central and Eastern Europe along Schachtian lines.

Thus by 1936, the structure of the monetary system had been transformed. The centrifugal forces inherent in divided control of the international monetary base, reinforced by political rivalries and economic nationalism born of depression and preparation for war, had finally triumphed over the tradition of fixed gold parities and the intention of statesmen to maintain them.

The formation of currency blocs with exchange rates flexible between them was regarded as pathological. The Western governments and the Western financial communities still yearned for the fixed parities of the gold standard, and currency blocs were closely associated with depression and protectionism. They might have become a method of mitigating monetary disorder in a world where there was more than one monetary center of gravity. But to a generation of bankers and economists steeped in the gold-standard tradition, the positive aspects of the new system were invisible.

IV. THE DOLLAR STANDARD AND ITS
TRANSFORMATION

N ations, like individuals, do not learn from experience unless experience is illuminated by sound theory. The attempt in the interwar period to restore an international monetary system based on fixed gold parities failed because control of the world's monetary base was divided. But the lesson that most postwar planners in Washington saw in this experience was simply that nations should eschew the manipulation of exchange rates and trade controls for national advantage. Exchange rates, they believed, should be solidly pegged, and countries' right to restrict trade should be narrowly circumscribed, except for normal tariffs. They attempted to construct a system of this kind without understanding its political preconditions. The blueprint agreed to at Bretton Woods in 1947 envisaged a multicurrency system, without any central control of world money. The projected International Monetary Fund was too weak, politically and in financial terms, to play that role.

Fortunately for the world, the United States emerged from the second world war in a position of unchallenged political and economic hegemony over Western Europe and Japan. As a result, the United States was able to establish a new, unified international monetary system based on the dollar, though with surprisingly little consciousness that it was doing so. John H. Williams, an early critic of Bretton Woods, seems to have been the only well-known American economist who foresaw that the dollar was destined to become the key currency of a global monetary system.

Nominally another version of the gold-exchange standard, the new system was not a multicurrency standard as the interwar system had been, but a single-currency (or key-currency) system. Sterling retained its status as a reserve currency within a reduced sterling area, but the pound was pegged to the dollar—not loosely, as in the 1930s, but tightly (after the 1949 devaluation). The sterling area thus became a subordinate monetary area within the general hegemony of the dollar rather than, as it had been in the 1930s, a more independent bloc. After 1949 the other Western European currencies were also tightly pegged to the dollar, as were the Canadian dollar and the Japanese yen. When, in 1959, the European currencies were made fully convertible into dollars on current account, the global dollar standard was fully established. For the next decade, the world enjoyed a degree of monetary order it had not known since 1913.

How the Federal Reserve Controlled
the World's Monetary Base

The mechanism by which the Federal Reserve controlled the world's monetary base and coordinated national monetary policies may best be understood in terms of a simplified example.

Suppose that the Federal Reserve stepped up its purchases of government securities, causing the U.S. money supply to accelerate sharply. The normal result would be an almost immediate net outflow of dollars from the United States to other countries; for, *ceteris paribus,* the speedup of money growth would produce a temporary excess supply of money in the United States relative to the demand for money (as compared with conditions in other countries). The resulting flow of dollars to other countries, when it was exchanged for local currency, would enlarge the local monetary base and provide the basis for a multiple expansion of the local money supply.

In principle, the local central bank might offset or sterilize the impact of the inflow on the monetary base by selling government securities, raising the commercial banks' required reserves, or cutting back its own loans and discounts to the banking system. Practically, however, its ability to do so was quite limited, essentially because its monetary system was small relative to the volume of dollars available to move in, in response to interest-rate and speculative incentives. The more money the local central bank mopped up, the greater would be the deficiency of money in the country relative to conditions in the United States. The result would be that the inflow of dollars would accelerate. Sterilization measures by the local central bank might nevertheless prove effective, at least in part, if applied with sufficient determination. But if that were done, the inflow of dollars would swell to such proportions as to threaten the stability of the country's exchange rate; for the large inflow would give rise to anticipations of an upvaluation, particularly in the case of a currency that was already considered strong, such as the German mark and some other continental European currencies.

Normally, therefore, the desire to avoid an upvaluation of its currency would cause the foreign central bank to adopt a policy parallel to the Federal Reserve's. Instead of trying to offset the impact of the inflow on the local monetary base, the authorities would take measures to speed the growth of the local monetary base—or allow the inflow of funds to have this effect—in order to slow down the inflow and ease the upward pressure on the exchange rate.

Conversely, when the U.S. money supply slowed down, the sequence was reversed. Funds were drawn from other countries to the United States, tending to reduce the other countries' monetary bases and to slow down the expansion of their money supplies. Again, the local authorities could, if they wished, have offset in part the domestic consequences of the outflow by conducting expansive open market operations or by easing reserve requirements. But to do so would have increased the relative excess of money in the country and accelerated the outflow. Evidently, a policy of this kind could not have been pursued for long, especially by a country whose currency was normally considered weak, for speculative outflows in anticipation of a devaluation would soon have exhausted the country's international reserves. Thus tight money in the United States forced other countries to tighten up too.

Owing to the size of the U.S. economy and the general use of the dollar as the principal reserve and intervention currency, changes in the rate of growth of the U.S. money supply, through their short-term effects on the capital account of the U.S. balance of payments, tended to force other countries to make parallel changes in their domestic money supplies in order to safeguard their international reserves or to protect the existing parities of their currencies.[2]

In a world where governments and central banks have assumed responsibility for full employment and where strong inflationary expectations have become endemic, the supply of international reserves must grow rather rapidly. Otherwise, countries wishing to maintain full employment will have to do so primarily by expanding the domestic component of the monetary base. In doing so, some of them will inevitably develop payments deficits which they will lack the international reserves to finance. In these circumstances, neither exchange-rate stability nor freedom of payments from exchange controls could long endure.

Where the largest country's currency serves as international reserves, as under the postwar dollar system, most other countries will try to arrange their exchange rates and conduct their domestic monetary policies so as to have persistent payments surpluses, in order to keep their reserves growing, while the key currency country itself will normally run a deficit. This imbalance is not a sign that the system is working badly. It reflects the fact that the central bank of the key currency country is forced, by the very structure of the system, to act as a kind of world central bank, responsible for the growth of the world's supply of base money.

Moreover, to make a system of this kind function well, the central bank of the key currency country has to follow a rather expansive monetary policy, as indeed the U.S. Federal Reserve did during the 1960s; for it must see to it that enough money is created not only to satisfy the domestic demand for money in the United States but also to supply a substantial part of the growth in the world's supply of base money. In this way, other countries can have their monetary cake and eat it too. They can safely allow their domestic money supplies to expand rapidly enough to assure reasonably full employment without endangering the stability of their exchange rates, while at the same time adding to their international reserves and enjoying the incidental luxury of chiding the key-currency country for its lack of balance-of-payments discipline.

Why the Dollar Standard Failed

If the besetting sin of a multicurrency standard with exchange rates fixed is its deflationary bias, that of a key currency system is its potential for inflation. It tends to inflation because there is no effective external brake on monetary expansion in the center country, and accordingly in the rest of the world. As long as the world believes that it can go on acquiring additional quantities of the key currency without incurring an exchange risk, there will be no effective balance-of-payments constraint on monetary expansion in the center country. Money creation by the center country is liable to get out of hand, if there are urgent reasons of national interest to allow this to happen.

Thus the dollar standard contained the seeds of its own destruction. Although the presumed immutability of the dollar's exchange rate was necessary to make the system work, it also proved to be the root cause of its downfall.

As long as Federal Reserve policy was heavily influenced by the desire to maintain domestic price stability, as was the case until 1965, the absence of external discipline of U.S. monetary policy did not threaten the system. But the shift in U.S. economic priorities that resulted from the Johnson Administration's decision to escalate the war in Vietnam changed the situation radically. Rapidly growing U.S. budget deficits led to increasingly rapid monetary expansion, with the result that money growth in other industrial countries was also forced to accelerate. As a result, the United States exported inflation to the rest of the world.

An important institutional development during the 1960s, the Eurodollar market, further increased the inflationary potential of the system. The Eurodollar market, with its large credit multiplier, amplified the system's ability to create base money on the foundation of any outflow of funds from the United States. The

Eurodollar market also provided a more convenient and accessible means for foreigners to finance short-term speculative positions against the dollar in European currencies. This, too, tended to enlarge European central banks' dollar reserves and monetary bases, when the dollar was under speculative pressure in the period 1971-1973. Central banks' practice of investing their dollar reserves in the Eurodollar market enlarged the credit multiplier of the system and accordingly its ability to create base money.

As luck would have it, the revelation of the dollar standard's inflationary potential came at a time when Western Europe had already grown restless about its subordinate political relationship with the United States and when the political detente with the Soviet Union gave European governments the freedom of action to express their desire for greater autonomy. The result was growing resistance to the dollar system. France led the resistance, as it had in the interwar period. The French government's outspoken critism of the dollar standard, its insistence on converting its dollar reserves into gold, and its call for a return to the gold standard, or something more like it, played a big part in undermining confidence in the dollar and setting off the series of currency crises that finally brought the dollar—and the system—down.

The enormous flows of speculative funds out of dollars and into European currencies and the yen that accompanied the breakdown further swelled the world's monetary base. Speculation against the dollar in 1971-1973 was highly inflationary. The dollar funds which moved across the exchanges enlarged the monetary base in Europe and Japan, but there was no corresponding reduction in the U.S. monetary base. This was partly because the Federal Reserve offset, by open market operations, the effect of any net outflows from the U.S. monetary system. Also, a large part of the new base money created in Europe and Japan had its origin in the Eurodollar market, as already noted. In the interwar period, by contrast, speculation against sterling in 1929-1930, against the dollar in 1931-1932, and against the French franc in 1934-1935 was deflationary rather than inflationary on a world scale because the country gaining reserves partly sterilized them. Also, there was no "offshore" banking system beyond the reach of national monetary authorities where base money could be created by the private demand for credit for currency speculation.

There are the reasons why the crisis of the dollar system unleashed a surge of inflation more violent than the modern world had ever known in peacetime. Just as the Great Depression contributed to protectionism and exchange control in the 1930s, so the dollar standard's legacy of inflation is having similar—though hopefully less extreme—consequences in our own time.

The New Dollar Standard

As in the 1930s, the breakdown of the old system has divided the world into currency blocs, with unstable, managed exchange rates between them. The largest is the dollar bloc. It is a residuum of the former global fixed-rate dollar system, including the Western Hemisphere and the Pacific countries. The Canadian dollar, though technically floating, is pegged de facto to the U.S. dollar by virtue of the exchange market's belief that the Canadian dollar will remain close to par with the American dollar. On the other side of the Atlantic, a continental European bloc, a successor to the former gold bloc, has formed. It consists of a group of lesser currencies that are pegged to the German mark—formally, under the European Community's common-float arrangement, or informally. The group includes the Belgian, Dutch, Austrian, and Scandinavian currencies and the Swiss franc—a group to which the French franc was also pegged, prior to its January 1974 float. On the outskirts of this bloc, the two weakest European currencies, the pound and the lira, float separately on a managed basis, while on the other side of the world, the yen moves unstably in a carefully managed float against the dollar. Exchange controls are everywhere on the rise and concern about a retreat into trade protectionism is growing.

In this new system, the position of the United States is different from that of the other industrial countries, as it was in the prewar system after 1936. The difference reflects the Federal

58

Reserve's superior ability to neutralize the effect of changes in the balance of payments on the U.S. monetary base—an ability that is due to the greater size of the U.S. economy as well as to the Fed's greater willingness and ability to use open market operations on a regular basis. As a result, the United States has more ability to control its exchange rate than the European monetary authorities have. If, for example, the U.S. Treasury and the Federal Reserve wish the dollar to depreciate, they can encourage the belief in the markets that the United States wants the dollar to fall and will do nothing to prevent it. Speculative movements of funds out of dollars and into other currencies will then weaken the dollar, for operators in the exchange markets are well aware that the European monetary authorities will not be able or willing to absorb the resulting large additions to their reserves and will have to let their currencies rise on the exchanges. This is, in fact, what happened in 1971. Similarly, the United States can, if it chooses, keep the dollar from appreciating by selling dollars on the exchange markets and preventing the rise in its reserves from affecting the U.S. monetary base through open market sales of securities.

The European governments have no analogous powers. If they seek to talk their currencies down against the dollar, the resulting outflow of speculative funds from their currencies into dollars will be more troublesome for them than for the United States. They will lose reserves and their monetary bases will contract, while the Federal Reserve will have no difficulty neutralizing the effect of the inflow of funds on the U.S. monetary base. Indeed, the Fed's curent practice of conducting open market operations in terms of growth targets for bank reserves and the money supply neutralizes automatically the domestic monetary effect of changes in the U.S. balance of payments. As a result, European countries must resort to exchange controls in order to assert their monetary autonomy vis-à-vis the United States. Unfortunately, such controls must be applied not only to exchange transactions with the dollar area but also to transactions within the European bloc; for a system of control that applied only to exchange transactions between the dollar and European currencies would be unworkable in the absence of close coordination of

European monetary policies—in effect, a European monetary union.

In sum, the international monetary system remains in essence a dollar system, with the dollar as the principal international money, but now with flexible rather than fixed rates among the leading currencies. The system resembles the interwar system after 1936. This time we shall have a chance to observe how a system of this kind works in the longer run.

V. A LOOK AHEAD

Two views on what to do about the current state of the international monetary system prevail today. Both are reflected in that ambiguous document, "First Outline of Reform", released at the September 1973 meeting of the International Monetary Fund (IMF). One view widely held in Europe seeks a return to relatively fixed exchange rates on a global basis, hoping to solve the problem of exchange-rate instability by giving to a committee of government representatives the right to determine whether and when exchange rates should be changed. The coordination of monetary policies would be accomplished by giving the IMF the right to issue financial assets—a new variety of special drawing right—which would be the sole or the principal component of international reserves.

This program presupposes a large measure of agreement among the principal powers on what constitutes an appropriate rate of expansion and pattern of distribution of international reserves. The exclusive power to create international reserves and to distribute them to central banks is, however, the power to determine the pace of money growth, business activity, and inflation in each of the countries participating in the system. How could governments, facing different domestic political demands and conditions, consistently agree on the appropriate pace of world money creation? How could they agree to delegate the authority to make such far-reaching decisions to a majority of their number? This approach to monetary reform simply overlooks the central political issue: how are national governments and monetary authorities to be induced to relinquish their right to control, or attempt to control, the national monetary base?

Moreover, an international reserve asset created in this manner could not achieve the status of a uniquely preferable asset for central banks, because it would be in competition with strong national currencies—such as the U.S. dollar and the German mark—for this role. Central banks would not agree to hold only or mainly the collectively created assets as reserves, since national currencies would at times be more attractive in terms of risk, yield, or convenience. The status that sterling and the dollar once enjoyed as the international reserve money par excellence cannot simply be conferred by agreement. It has to be earned in practice and confirmed by long experience.

A second reform program, which enjoys general support in the United States, stresses the shortcomings of the first view and pins its hopes on the "adjustment process"—i.e., on flexible exchange rates. Proponents of this view are so impressed by the dangers of fixed exchange rates—particularly their vulnerability to speculation and their potential for deflation or inflation—that the analogous weaknesses of a flexible-rate system are overlooked. Proponents of flexibility argue that, with exchange rates responsive to market forces, countries would be free to pursue whatever monetary policy they wish. If this results in a rate of monetary expansion that is out of step with the rest of the world, the exchange rate will simply rise or fall; unless the central bank intervenes in the exchange markets, no net inflows or outflows of funds need take place. Large scale exchange speculation would also be prevented.

All this is undeniably so, but the conclusion that exchange-rate flexibility is the royal road to monetary order does not follow. In the first place, the movement of the exchange rate resulting from differences in domestic and external monetary conditions is by no means a matter of indifference for countries of small and medium size, where the ratio of tradeable goods and services to the gross national product is high—a category which includes all the industrial countries except Japan and the United States. If the country pursues a more restrictive monetary policy than the rest of the world, its exchange rate will rise, and the competitive impact on exporting and import-competing industries may be severe; for there is no assurance that, with national monetary policies uncoordinated, exchange rates will normally stay close to their purchasing power parities. If the country pursues a more expansive monetary policy than other countries, its exchange rate may fall and there may be upward pressure on the domestic price level, aggravating any price inflation already present.

Thus the country may find that, for much of the time, its freedom to follow its own monetary course is more apparent than real. If its monetary policy fails to conform to monetary conditions abroad, it may import too much inflation or suffer too much foreign competition. To avoid these problems, it would have to conduct its monetary policy much as if it were in a fixed-rate regime, conforming its policy to that of the rest of the world. This is the main reason why, when a global monetary system breaks down, currency blocs form. Smaller countries need exchange-rate stability more than large countries. Thus they are inclined to peg their currencies to that of the larger power with which they have the closest trade and financial ties.

As for exchange speculation, it is true that flexible exchange rates can prevent large speculative flows across the exchanges; but they cannot prevent the speculative buying and selling of currencies from greatly exaggerating the movement of exchange rates, with politically unacceptable consequences for competitive positions or price levels. The behavior of exchange rates since the abandonment of fixed parities between the dollar and European currencies and the yen has rudely shaken economists' faith in the stability of flexible exchange rates. Economists have learned the hard way that unless underlying conditions are conducive to rate stability—in particular, unless national monetary policies are coordinated—destabilizing exchange speculation is likely to cause wide swings in flexible exchange rates from time to time. Even the U.S. Treasury seems to have lost some of its earlier faith in flexibility, now that the dollar is appreciating.

Flexible exchange rates do not alter fundamentally the problem of international monetary order. Order does not depend on the exchange-rate regime but on the presence or absence of central control of the world's monetary base.

These negative conclusions about the two principal proposals for structural reform of the international monetary system suggest that the system will probably continue indefinitely in about its present form, for the system of blocs along with several separately managed floating currencies that came into being spontaneously after the dollar's fall from grace reflects accurately enough contemporary political and economic realities. In present circumstances, there is no possibility of restoring a fixed-rate single-currency standard, or its functional equivalent, that could create the conditions of monetary order on a global basis. The best that can be hoped for is that the present complex pattern will in time evolve into a system of well-organized blocs, within which the conditions of monetary order will be achieved in tolerable degree and which will manage to avoid trade and exchange-rate warfare with each other.

One can envisage a system consisting of two or three monetary blocs, organized around the United States, the European Community, and perhaps Japan. Within each bloc, monetary conditions would be coordinated naturally, so to speak, by virtue of the use of the leading currency as key currency on a regional scale. In the case of the European Community, monetary control might conceivably be exercised by a supranational central bank. Between the blocs, exchange rates would be managed flexibly, and intervention policies would be negotiated on a basis of political equality.

A system of this kind would probably be less problematic than the present system, because of its greater political symmetry. Each of the blocs would be large enough to enjoy substantial monetary autonomy; its monetary base would be large relative to potential inflows and outflows of funds, so that their monetary effects could be neutralized. Each bloc would be able to exert as much influence as the other bloc or blocs over their exchange rates with each other. The blocs would accordingly be able to bargain as equals over intervention policy and the appropriate level of exchange rates. Such a monetary system would according-ly be less prone to disintegration and conflict than the present system, although its success in this regard would also depend on the general state of political relationships among the United States, Western Europe, and Japan.

Unfortunately, however, this model is not much closer to present possibilities than the two proposals for international monetary reform discussed earlier. The closest approximation to it is the dollar area, particularly the relationship between Canada and United States, where the Canadian dollar is stabilized relative to the U.S. dollar by the exchange market's self-fulfilling expectation that the two currencies will stay close to parity with each other, and where exchange control is therefore unnecessary. The Latin American currencies are and will presumably remain pegged to the U.S. dollar: some of them such as the Brazilian cruziero and the Colombian peso, on sliding pegs; others, like the Mexican peso, the Venezuelan bolivar, and the Central American and Caribbean currencies, with fixed parities. The same is true of a number of Pacific and Far Eastern currencies, including the Australian and New Zealand dollars and a few other currencies such as the South African rand. All these members of the dollar area will continue to use the dollar as their principal reserve asset. Unlike Canada, however, most of them will make extensive use of exchange controls, as they traditionally have. Thus the dollar area is hardly a model of monetary order, though it is more orderly than the monetary system as a whole.

Western Europe is the main problem area. In present circumstances, there is no European country whose currency can serve as the principal reserve asset of a regional key-currency system. In strictly economic terms, the German mark is the logical candidate. The German economy is Europe's largest and the German currency one of Europe's strongest, while Germany's smaller Western European neighbors already peg their currencies de facto to the mark. Germany lacks one traditional requirement of a key currency—a well developed domestic financial center with strong international links. But there would be nothing to prevent a large, efficient offshore DM market from developing in London and other major European financial centers—growing out of the present Euro-DM market—if its development were stimulated by the use of the mark as an official reserve currency in Europe and if exchange controls within the Common Market were eliminated. Be that as it may, acceptance of Germany's monetary leadership would be out of the question, politically, for France and Britain.

Britain has in abundance the financial institutions as well as the tradition of monetary leadership. But sterling is and will continue to be periodically weak, due to the British economy's low potential growth rate which, coupled with an unswerving dedication to full employment, results in a chronic tendency to excessive domestic monetary expansion. Continental European central bankers have memories that stretch back to 1931; they are not likely again to consider sterling an attractive reserve asset.

More generally, France, Germany, and Britain are too nearly equal in size and status and too jealous of each other to make a regional system based on the monetary leadership of one of them possible. Thus hopes for monetary order on a European scale must be pinned to the possibility of achieving monetary union. By "monetary union" is meant a more or less supranational European monetary authority that is able to control the growth of the monetary base throughout the European Community. Yet while that may be possible one day, it seems remote at the present time; for the three larger members of the Community are not likely in the foreseeable future to be willing or politically able to delegate such far-reaching control over their economic life to a common authority.

The Community's present monetary arrangement—the common float or, colloquially, the "snake"—pegs the Community currencies (except sterling, the Irish pound, and the lira) to each other at official parities, with a small margin allowed between the strongest and the weakest currency. The member currencies as a group are managed flexibly against outside currencies, mainly by the purchase or sale of dollars by the German central bank. The currencies participating in the arrangement are kept in line with each other by the member central banks buying or selling each other's currencies. The central banks keep small reserves in the main member currencies and may also borrow from each other, within narrow limits, to obtain the currencies meeded for such intervention.

Thus in its present form the European bloc is a multicurrency system on a regional scale. As such, it is prone to the difficulties already explained. Since it lacks means of coordinating the members' monetary policies, particularly as between the two major participants, France and Germany, it is bound to run into difficulties. Its brief history (it was established in its present form in February 1973) has been punctuated by currency crises, arising in large part out of differences between French and German monetary policies. The members of the arrangement have found it necessary, in order to keep their currencies in line, to tighten periodically their exchange controls. The controls apply not only to transactions with outside countries but also with other members. Thus the arrangement, far from advancing the cause of European economic integration, has moved the Community in the opposite direction. It is not likely to be abandoned, however. For all its shortcomings the float remains an important symbol of Europe's search for "identity"—of European hopes for ultimate unity. The only alternative—flexible rates among the participating currencies, or more realistically between the mark group and the French franc—would divide Europe politically. The snake is likely to survive, though its future will not be less troubled than its past.

(France's decision to take the fanc out of the European currency snake and float it "temporarily", announced January 19, 1974, came after this report was completed. It tends to confirm the above prognosis. The snake has survived the trauma though in truncated form. It is now a cluster of lesser Continental currencies that are pegged to the mark by the German central bank's buying or selling them against marks. Coming at a time of severe balance-of-payments strain on European currencies and deep divisions on oil policy within the European Community, this new demonstration of the Community's institutional short-comings and political weakness bodes ill for its future.)

Britain and Italy will doubtless remain on their present independent monetary courses, because the only alternative—joining the common float—would be worse. With their chronic domestic economic and political troubles, these two countries are particularly poor candidates for membership in a multicurrency system with fixed exchange rates. Japan, too, will doubtless continue to go its separate way, with the yen loosely pegged to the dollar and with extensive use of exchange controls to help manage its balance of payments.

How Well Will It Work?

This, then, is the most probable structure of the international monetary system for the foreseeable future. How well or how badly will it work? In the 1930s a similar system worked badly, in the sense that disintegrative forces were predominant. Efforts to protect domestic economies from the consequences of worldwide deflation led to high tariffs and other barriers to imports, as well as to exchange controls to protect reserves. The autarchic economic policies pursued for military reasons by Germany and Japan added to the disintegration.

On the other hand, there is little evidence in the historical record of the beggar-my-neighbor exchange-rate policies that are commonly supposed to have characterized the 1930s. Actually, the leading countries followed circumspect exchange-rate policies. Major exchange-rate changes in this period were mainly forced by internal or external developments. The pound's devaluation in 1931 and subsequent steep decline was forced by strong speculative pressure against a currency generally believed to be overvalued. After the dollar was devalued in 1934, the pound returned to about its pre-1931 relationship with the dollar and remained in that vicinity until the eve of World War II. Britain managed the exchange rate of the pound after 1931 with an eye to avoiding conflict with, and possible retaliation by, the United States (see Pumphrey, 1942: 809ff.).

The French franc's decline in 1935-1936 was forced by the dollar's devaluation and by domestic developments in France, particularly the expansive fiscal and monetary policies of the Popular Front government and the resulting capital flight. From 1937 on, the franc remained close to its 1937 level vis-à-vis both the dollar and the pound (it was pegged to the pound in 1938), until the approach of war forced it down. On the other hand, the dollar's managed downward float in 1933 and subsequent formal devaluation in 1934 were deliberate acts of policy rather than forced decisions. Domestic objectives—the desire to push up U.S. commodity prices—were uppermost in the minds of President Roosevelt and his advisers. But after March 1934, the dollar was back on a fixed gold parity and no longer subject to manipulation by the authorities. Thus the conventional picture of the 1930s as a time of unbridled competitive depreciation of currencies is a gross exaggeration, to say the least. It is probably a construct of postwar Keynesian economics, projected back on the 1930s, as Sidney E. Rolfe and James Burtle (1973: c. 4) have recently suggested.

Nevertheless, the present state of the system is hardly encouraging. For several years at least, the industrial countries will be struggling to bring inflation under control, with varying degrees of determination and success. Marked divergences of monetary policies and rates of inflation are accordingly likely. Major adjustments of trade balances and international invest-ments flows, resulting from earlier exchange-rate changes, will also be going on. The large resulting swings in exchange rates will be amplified at times by destabilizing speculation.

In these circumstances, governments and central banks will face the problem of preventing exchange-rate movements from undermining their domestic objectives. When, for example, they are fighting inflation with tight money and their exchange rates rise, the impact on export and import-competing industries and on employment will be far from welcome, particularly when domestic unemployment rises. They may resist the rise or accelerate the decline of their exchange rates by "inward" exchange controls, and may be strongly tempted to raise barriers against imports and to subsidize exports. When, conversely, a country eases monetary policy, the resulting downward pressure on the exchange rate, reinforced perhaps by exchange specula-tion, may cause domestic inflation to accelerate, creating the temptation to check the depreciation of the currency by "outward" exchange control and import restrictions.

Militating against these temptations are the risks of retaliation and the habits of international cooperation built up over the last 25 years. The commitments of the members of the European Community to each other, the established rules of the General Agreement on Tariffs and Trade, as well as Europe's and Japan's remaining military dependence on the United States, have the same effect. Such powerful political constraints on international economic disintegration were not present in the 1930s. On the contrary, the industrial world was divided into hostile ideological camps, the United States was in an isolationist mood, and there were no agreed rules inhibiting resort to trade barriers. Then, too, mass unemployment was probably a more compelling incentive to impose import barriers than are recessions or inflations today, particularly in a world where the international integration of markets has much stronger political support than it had in the 1930s.

The immediate danger is that the rapid improvement of the U.S. balance of payments—due in part to the steep rise in the world price of oil—will put so much downward pressure on the European currencies and the yen that Europe and Japan, already suffering from politically intolerable inflation, may feel compelled to restrict imports as well as to tighten exchange controls, in order to stem their currencies' fall. The alternative of large scale intervention in the exchange markets to support their currencies against the dollar is limited by their international reserves—or their willingness to borrow dollars from the Federal Reserve and the Fed's willingness to lend. Then, too, such support makes it more difficult for Europe and Japan to expand their monetary bases, which these countries will soon feel compelled to do in order to cope with stagnant or falling output and rising unemployment. In these circumstances, the temptation to some countries not only to limit outward capital flows but also to control imports could become overwhelming.

In sum, the prospects for greater international monetary order are hardly bright, but a far-reaching disintegration of the international economic system such as occurred in the 1930s is not likely. The industrial countries have strong common interests in avoiding that outcome. This is true, at any rate, so long as their fundamental political ties—the European Community, the Atlantic alliance, and the U.S.-Japan security treaty—endure. In the last analysis, international economic order depends more on the substructure of political order than on trade and monetary arrangements.

NOTES

1. As John M. Keynes (1925) had prophesied in his The Economic Consequences of Mr. Churchill.

2. Statistical evidence of synchronization of changes in the rate of growth of the money supply in the United States, Britain, and Germany in the 1960s may be found in Cleveland (1972: 410-411).

REFERENCES

BROWN, W. A. (1974) The International Gold Standard Reinterpreted, 1914-1934. New York

BURTLE, J. and S. E. ROLFE, (1973) The Great Wheel: The World Monetary System, a Reinterpretation. New York

CLEVELAND, H. van B. (1972) "Reflections on international monetary order." Columbia Jouranl of Transnational Law (Fall): 410-411.

KEYNES, J. M. (1925) The Economic Consequences of Mr. Churchill. London

PUMPHREY, L. M. (1942) "The exchange equalization account of Great Britain, 1932-1939." American Exchange Review (December): 809 ff.

SKIDELSKY, R. (1973) Issues in British Monetary Policy. Unpublished paper prepared for The Lehrman Institute. New York (November)

INTERNATIONAL RELATIONS/CURRENT AFFAIRS
$2.50/£1.00

The Washington Papers

... intended to meet the need for authoritative, yet prompt, public appraisal of the major changes in world affairs.

Commissioned and written under the auspices of the Center for Strategic and International Studies (CSIS), Georgetown University, Washington, D.C., and published for CSIS by SAGE Publications, Beverly Hills/London.

Strains in International Finance and Trade

This Washington Paper presents two timely studies on issues of international trade and finance. Sanderson analyzes the impact of the energy crisis on U.S.–European economic relations within a generalized discussion of long- and short-term policy problems. Cleveland examines the underlying assumptions of the contemporary and international context of international monetary problems. Combined, these studies contribute much to an understanding of the current strain in the international economic system.

Fred H. Sanderson

Fred H. Sanderson has served in the State Department since 1946, most recently as a member of the planning and Coordination Staff. He has also served as Chief of the Division of Research for Western Europe, Finance Adviser in the U.S. Mission to the OECD, Director of the Office of Food Programs, and Deputy Executive Director of the President's Commission on International Trade and Investment Policy.

Harold van B. Cleveland

Harold van B. Cleveland is Vice President, International Economics, of the First National City Bank. He was formerly associated with the U.S. Department of State, with the Committee for Economic Development as Assistant Director of Research, and with the John Hancock Mutual Life Insurance Company of Boston as Counsel. Before joining Citibank he was Director of Atlantic Policy Studies of the Council on Foreign Relations in New York. He is the author of two books and numerous articles on international economic problems.